PIP
THE SCAREDY-CAT DUCK

PIP
THE SCAREDY-CAT DUCK

Grace and Max Lyons
Illustrated by Sara Edmondson

© 2015 Jill Olsen. All rights reserved.

Trusted Books is an imprint of Deep River Books. The views expressed or implied in this work are those of the author. To learn more about Deep River Books, go online to www.DeepRiverBooks.com.

No part of this publication may be reproduced, stored in a retrieval system or transmitted in any way by any means—electronic, mechanical, photocopy, recording or otherwise—without the prior permission of the Publisher, except as provided by USA copyright law.

ISBN 13: 978-1-63269-163-7
Library of Congress Catalog Card Number: 2015931783

DEDICATION

With heartfelt thanks to Dad and Mom
for all your love and care.

We love you more than
chocolate-iced cakes.

At 3:55 one spring afternoon, Max and Grace began their usual walk home from school, two ordinary kids on an ordinary day. But adventure awaited that would quickly turn ordinary into extra, extra-ordinary.

"Hey! What's that?" Grace shouted, pointing toward a yellow shape bobbing up and down in the stream. She crinkled her face and squeezed her eyes nearly shut, like she'd done a hundred times playing baseball on a sunny day.

Max stopped in his tracks and dared his sister to prove she saw anything special. "It's probably just a silly old piece of cork," he said.

"It's much too big for that," said Grace. "But it's no bigger than a rubber ducky."

Max agreed. As a matter of fact, the shape looked *exactly* like a rubber ducky, except for one thing. "It's ALIVE!"

Gasp!!!

The kids raced to the edge of the water just in time to see the beak, of what looked like a baby chick, scrape up against a rock. He went under, sputtering and peeping.

"He's drowning!" Grace shouted. "We have to do something, Max! Help!"

Max stood with his hands on his hips. He looked upstream. Then he looked downstream. Nothing moved except for a few blackbirds rustling the leaves. No mother in sight. "There's nothing we can do," he said. "We can't catch him. He's too fast!"

"And all alone," Grace added. "Come on!" she shouted, as she raced past Max toward home. "There's no time to waste!"

Within minutes, Mom Lyons had driven them back to the stream. She whipped her SUV up under the trees. Grace tumbled out, leaving the door open for Max, who followed quickly behind, shoebox in hand. Mom brought up the rear, kicking her shoes off as she ran.

"There he is!"

The rescuers hurried to surround the little guy just in time to see his head pop up.

The current was fast, but not too fast for Max! He steadied himself on a slippery rock, set his sights on the bobbing baby, and plunged into the knee-deep stream.

"YEOW!!! Is that all the thanks I get?"

No doubt, Max had scooped up more than sandy water. "Did you see that? He bit me! Ungrateful thing. Here, YOU carry him!"

"Gladly. Poor thing." Grace took the lid off the soggy box as she slid into the back seat of the car.

Wide-eyed and wet, the downy chick showed his face.

"Aw, look," said Grace. "He's so cute!" Mom nodded and smiled as she backed the car out onto the road. The hero sat with his arms crossed, forcing himself not to pay attention to all the "cuteness."

Once home, Grace tucked the shoebox under her arm like a football and ran straight upstairs.

Max went, too, shouting out a new question on every other step. "Where are we going to keep a baby chick? What will we feed him? How can we possibly take care of an animal that needs to live on a farm?"

"A farm? Nana grew up on a farm in Iowa! Max, you're brilliant."

"Mom! Call Nana!" Grace bellowed from around the corner. "She'll know what to do!"

"Take it easy, little fella. You'll be safe here." The chick protested loudly as Grace guided him out of the box and into the bathtub.

Meanwhile Mom put Nana on speakerphone. "You say you rescued him from a stream? What color is he?" Max and Grace listened as Mom described the newest member of the family. "Well, how do you know it's a chick?" Nana asked. "Have you looked at his feet?"

Max pushed past Grace and leaned over the side of the tub. His eyes almost popped out of his head.

"Our chick is a duck!!!"

Grace peered over the edge to see for herself. "Sure enough! It's a duck—all the way from his head to his webbed feet!"

"Mom! Tell Nana it's a duck!" Grace yelled from upstairs pulling Max into the hallway.

"What does a baby duck eat?" Max shrugged.

But Nana knew. Corn. Corn meal, corn muffins, anything corn.

 They ransacked the pantry, searching for anything that resembled corn. "What about corn chips?" Max asked.

Grace shook her head and reported, "No luck, Nana! What's next?"

Nana came up with a plan that got the kids excited. Mom helped gather a bowl for water and one for dried oatmeal. Then Grace ran to get something extra comfy for the bottom of the tub.

Was it shag carpet? Or a blanket? No . . .

It was grass!

Never had a rescued duck seen such luxury.

After final hugs and sweet dream wishes, Grace flipped the light switch. "Night, night," she said. "Don't let the bed bugs bite."

Not one for tucking in ducks, Max turned and quietly closed the door behind him.

PEEP! PEEP! PEEP! PEEP! PEEP! PEEP! PEEP!!!

The cries of a baby duck afraid of the dark echoed out from under the bathroom door!

The kids had no sooner crawled under the covers than they were up again, calling out for help.

"What's all the fuss?" Mom asked, as she burst into Max's room.

"Pleeeeeease, do something about all that peeping!" said Max. He covered his tired, yawning face with a pillow.

Mom gathered up the baby duck and nestled into the living room sofa to watch the news.

She held him up against her chest with both hands cupped around his shaking, little body.

"What's your name, little fella? Aren't you tired? I know I am." Soon his eyes drooped shut and his body relaxed. And so did Mom's.

The whole family fell asleep thinking of a good name for a rescued duck who was afraid of the dark . . . and afraid to be alone.

Morning came and two sleepy kids plunked down at the breakfast table.

"What about Pip?" Grace asked. "That could be a good name."

Max pondered. "Like, short for 'peep'?"

"As in 'PEEPING'!" Grace said. The kids giggled and nodded in agreement.

Grace gently tapped the beak of the noisy wonder next to her on the table. "Peeping. It's what Pip does best."

PEEP! PEEP! PEEP! PEEP! PEEP! PEEP! PEEP!

Time had come for Pip to know he wasn't the family's only pet. Destin and Boise strained against their collars to get a close-up look at the newest addition.

Pip froze.

Max imitated Pip's peeping. "Peep! Peep! Peep! Is that all you ever do? You're probably thinking, 'Are you my mom? Are you my mom?' No way, Pip. Their ears are too long, and they have too many legs!"

Grace scooped up Pip.

"Don't worry, Pip. I've got you. Hey, you're just in time for the family's Easter photo shoot!"

With Pip in hand and the camera ready, everyone prepared to pose. Everyone, that is, except for the dogs. They were not very happy wearing fuzzy bunny ears. And particularly unhappy about their fuzzy, new brother, Pip!

After lots of pawing and pouting, the group settled down for one last picture. Pip, the Easter Darling Duck, was here to stay.

Every day Pip spent in the Lyons' tub was followed by a night of peep, peep, peeping.

Max began to wonder why he had rescued Pip in the first place.

Until one day, an invitation came from Ms. Crane, Max's teacher. She wanted the whole class to meet Pip, and it happened to be Max's turn for Show-and-Tell. Perfect.

When Max heard the news, he seemed a little uncertain. "What if he starts peeping, and I can't get him to stop?" Mom encouraged him in her gentle way. "It will be fine," she said. "You'll see. It might even be fun!"

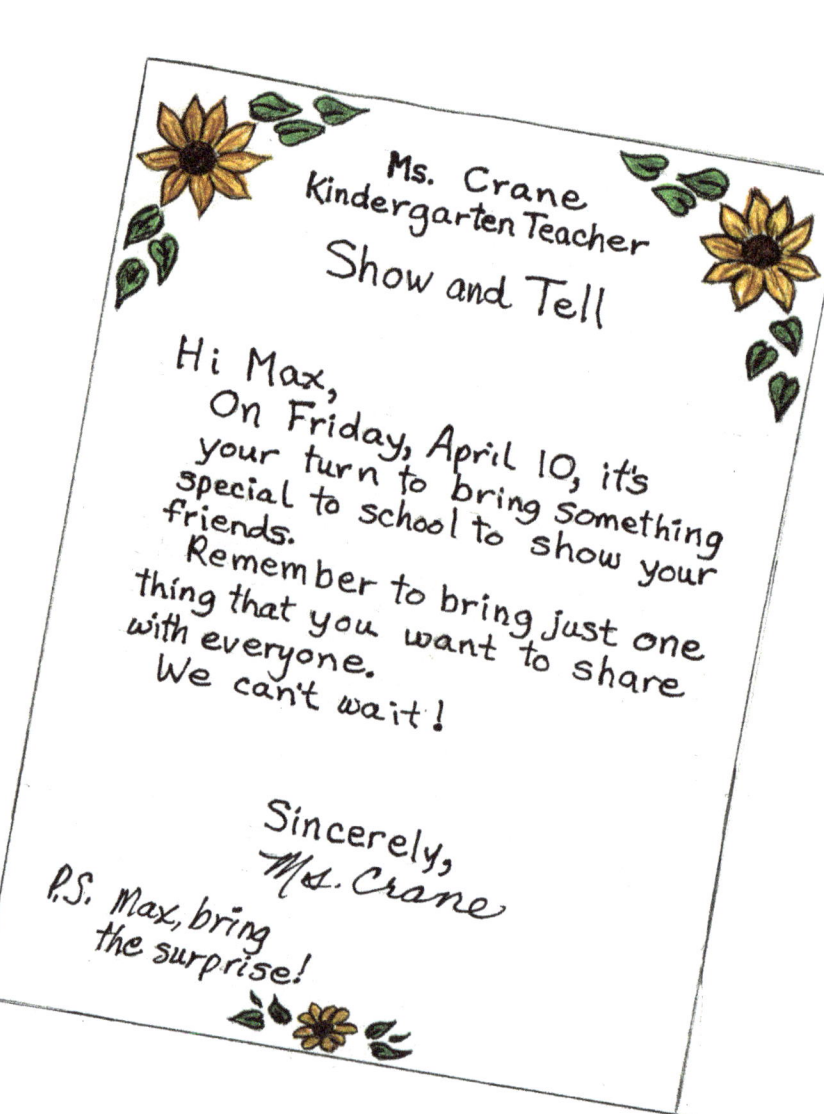

Ms. Crane
Kindergarten Teacher
Show and Tell

Hi Max,
On Friday, April 10, it's your turn to bring something special to school to show your friends.
Remember to bring just one thing that you want to share with everyone.
We can't wait!

Sincerely,
Ms. Crane

P.S. Max, bring the surprise!

And it was! The whole class could see and hear that Show-and-Tell was going to be special.

PEEP! PEEP!
PEEP! PEEP! PEEP!
PEEP! PEEP!

Max choked back a giggle as Ms. Crane did her best to seat everyone knee to knee in the reading circle. She didn't want Max's two-legged surprise to escape!

What Max didn't know was that Ms. Crane had a two-legged surprise of her own!

A baby chick, fresh from the farm!

Ms. Crane lifted her downy friend from his cage and set him in the center of the circle.

He stared up at Pip.

Pip stared back.

But not for long.

PEEP! PEEP! PEEP! PEEP! PEEP!

"Look at the scaredy cat!" someone yelled. Everybody laughed as Pip ran for cover.

When the chaos calmed, Ms. Crane invited Max to take his place in her special chair.

"Come on, little guy," Max said. "Everyone, this is Pip. It's short for 'peep,' as in PEEPING!" The class roared. Max beamed.

"We haven't always known what he was. In fact, when we found him sputtering and peeping in the stream, we didn't even know he was a duck!" Max went on to tell the tale of Pip's daring rescue, from the beginning to the end. The class cheered. Max whispered to his peeping scaredy-cat, "This was the best Show-and-Tell day ever!"

Indeed it was.

And because of it, Pip, the scaredy-cat duck, became quite the star. Kids from school flocked to the Lyons' home for a chance to hold him.

Many of the moms smiled at Ms. Lyons in "Mom Code." They nodded and shot their best "I'm-glad-it's-you-and-not-me" looks.

But mom was proud of Pip and his rescuing heroes. She invited everyone out for a little fun in the back yard. "Pictures and playtime!" she called out.

PEEP! PEEP! PEEP!

Never had a rescued duck seen such pampering!

"Peep, peep, peep! Is that all you ever do?" Max giggled and scooped up Pip.

"I'm so glad we saved you!"

"Me, too!" said Grace. And the trio leaned in for a special photo op.

PEEP! PEEP! PEEP! PEEP! PEEP! PEEP! PEEP!

The crowd erupted!

Thanks to two ordinary kids with extraordinary love and a sense of adventure, Pip, the scaredy-cat duck, was no longer afraid . . .

And no longer alone . . .

Grace and Max found Pip the perfect home!

A NOTE FROM GRACE AND MAX

Some of you might think putting a scaredy-cat duck in a tub is a crazy thing to do, especially a duck with such a peep as Pip's. You're probably right, but rescuing Pip turned into an amazing adventure we wouldn't trade for anything. As Mom would say, in spite of the stinky tub and messy shirts, "It was all good."

Caring for one of God's special creatures helped us learn we can make a difference in our world—big or small—even when we're young. We never dreamed we would be called heroes for such a simple thing as rescuing a duck. We're just ordinary kids. Now we know that being a hero just means responding to others in need, even when it might not be easy.

With love, a sense of adventure, and a willingness to help, you, too, can be a hero! How? Just look around your neighborhood or your school and be ready to serve anyone who needs help. If you want more ideas, we brainstormed with Nana and put our thoughts in a list for you on the next page. And visit our website (**www.CanYouBeAHero.com**) where we can share stories and challenge each other to be everyday H.E.R.O.E.S. (Helping Everyone Reach Others with Extraordinary Service). And you can also read . . . **"The Rest of the Story . . ."**

When you start looking for ways to be a hero, adventure will find you—trust us. You'll be part of some great stories that we can't wait to hear. Thanks for reading ours!

Grace and Max Lyons

JOIN THE ADVENTURE: BE A HERO!

Choose an activity, grab a friend or gather your family, and let your adventure begin!

1. Volunteer at an animal rescue shelter.

2. Adopt a nearby mile of road by picking up litter.

3. Host a food drive and donate it to a local homeless shelter.

4. Have a garage sale to sell your extra toys and stuff. Give the profits to your favorite charity or to a family in need.

5. Start a Kids-Helping-Kids Homework Club.

6. Write letters to men and women serving in the military.

7. Volunteer as a buddy on a sports team for boys and girls with special needs.

8. Fill boxes at a local food bank.

9. Read stories, sing songs, or do crafts at a retirement center.

10. Think of your own thing and make a difference in someone else's life!

To share your stories or for other ideas, including a list of great causes and organizations, visit our website at
www.CanYouBeAHero.com

THE REAL PIP FAMILY

www.ingramcontent.com/pod-product-compliance
Lightning Source LLC
Chambersburg PA
CBHW061128070526
44584CB00033B/4263